LAST RITES

LAST RITES

CHRISTOPHER BUCKLEY

ITHACA HOUSE

Grateful acknowledgment is due the editors of the following magazines in which these poems first appeared: Calavera Press *6 poems, Ironwood, Seneca Review, The Missouri Review, New England Review, Pebble, Cutbank, The Chowder Review, California Quarterly, Quarry West, Spectrum, Skywriting, The Black Warrior Review, The Louisville Review, Green House, Graham House Review, San Marcos Review, Sun & Moon, Scree, Big Moon, Bachy, Santa Barbara Magazine*.

The publication of this book is made possible with public funds from the New York State Council on the Arts.

ITHACA HOUSE
108 North Plain Street
Ithaca, New York 14850

Ithaca House books are distributed by
SBD
1606 Ocean View Ave.
Kensington, CA 94707

Library of Congress Cataloging in Publication Data

Buckley, Christopher, 1948-
    Last Rites.

    Poems.
    I. Title.
PS3552.U339L3   811'.54   80-12937
ISBN 0-87886-109-2

CONTENTS

for Glover, Dennis, and Diane

I. CALIFORNIA

It begins with no one to speak to
and traces of sky vague as skim milk;
it continues with the too-green ivy and mint
crowding the door, forcing it ajar. . .

I take a drive up Coast Highway 1
and the ocean's dusty glare blinds
the rear-view mirror and passes through me
as l pass through four, five, o'clock;
at Portuguese Bend I pull over and park.

At the point, Lloyd Wright's church
quavers with the break and undertow of waves;
its 50' tower is a marker for the lost.
The abandoned houses tilt with the steady withdrawal
of God's hand from the cliffs. Once I swam out, dove,
listened, heard nothing, and was given no sign
but the kelp slipping through my hands like beads.
More than once I have mentioned how I feel--
how it is these houses have had to love themselves.

In the vacant living rooms and atriums
I imagine the lives that went on, almost see them
like moonlight faint on the salt particles of air.
I imagine the years let go and the people
sealed in blank envelopes of heart,
and stop asking how we've held together and what for.

Spent most of the day
finding this canyon stream,
lungs popping, rasping
in this thin hot air.
Even as I rest, the sun
comes back at me,
and at this height
windows of resorts blink
like the eyes of snakes.

In Cathedral City
my mother looks for
wild flowers in the wash
that fronts her house.
She finds only a few petals
of shade beneath some stone.
Her hands are blanched
as upturned roots and
there will be no one
to look for her
when I have gone. She shakes
her head slowly when I say
this state will turn to sand
and ride the ocean out.
Even now there are not
many sparrows remaining
in the oleander trees.

Night arrives on the air
without a wind to stir

the dust. At the corner
of the valley,
one hawk fans the heat.
Stars and the thousand
lights turn red.
in my sunburned eyes.
A full moon rises
where this stream begins
and pours like salt.

6 *COYOTE FIRE*

for Glover Davis

Cinders falling
the light turns orange--
oak bark popped,
deer hooves on asphalt.
I saw spring grass
go in a thick sweat.
We soaked the house
and when the fire line
jumped we scrambled
for the last open road.
In the rolling smoke
I heard water hiss
from a pine. A flight
of doves sobbed toward
the sea.
          First light--
I found my house
like a white dot
on a black die.
Heat rushed from
the charred foundation
of the tool shed.
Grease of the coyote's paw
on the buckled hood of a car,
fur stuck to the melted glass.
From the blistered creek
the gold pump
of a pheasant's wings
rose like ash--everything
delivered to the air.

At the Museum of Natural History
nuns led us in single file to see
stone bowls, hooks and totems from whale,
photos of painted caverns beneath the falls.
Chumash gathered black mustard, acorn,
cactus apple, and toward the end, fish.
Snowy Egret and Blue Teal whistled
over the lagoon, guiding by stars.
No one said how all at once
the Chumash died. At the Mission
padres preserve their bones and
medicine sticks like a dead child's toys.

What is now Coal Oil Point
was a village of fifty boatmen.
Fathers returned there from the nets
singing of their catch--
singing the tongues of fish,
the hands of water, singing
how they take only those
with no pain in their eyes.

Evening gathers and the lagoon
rinses a copper film along the shore.
I look for soapstone, seal bones,
any relic washed out of life--
I go where gulls no longer squawk
or scavenge and find little
but clots of tar, blood berries
of Madrone fallen from the cliff.

On one rock the fossil of a scallop
outlines a face--the nose broken,
the eyes sunk past light--
and the white half of a moon
floats on its side like a fish.

for Jon and Gary, May 24, 1975

Already the light is gone in the groom's cabin,
the folding chairs are stacked or teetering
against tables like the few remaining guests--
the moon starts to eclipse, goes red as cabernet
and then disappears.
                    The best man, lifting
at least his fifth bottle of champagne,
stands on a table in his white tuxedo;
and turning slowly toward us, like Tommy Dorsey
to the band, invites us to toast the moon,
the clear Fresno moon, which he finds is gone.
He drinks and then proposes the million moons
rising in the grapes of the San Joaquin.
I am the only one to find my feet, weaving
like an ash tree in wind. He comes over
and tells me how his Estonian grandmother drank
on her wedding day, took care of his grandfather,
and returned to drink with anyone that was left.
He looks to his glass and the bubbles spin
like the wheel of stars going loose over his head.
I help him to his car where he takes off stiff shoes,
puts on his sneakers, and offers to show me
the night-empty road; says he's going to walk it off
and come back for more. He says, "When the moon
shows a fingernail, I'll open another bottle,
no one should have to find their way alone."

California 1977

Early sun, dollop of blood dying high white,
a sky off-blue as thistle spikes--our hearts start
with coffee, amber lawns, the little mist that rises.

The drought shocked blossoms out like never before--
oleanders hang bruised and dolorous in their
                                        profusion.
I watch the lantana's showy heads break loose
into a thousand cornets announcing nothing.

The calendar frames this date, August 15, in red:
The Assumption and a holy day of obligation.
Pools of shade suck up; dark lines of women
dissolve from mass into the bright distance.

By the beach, the unctuous stream of Mercedes thins;
and oil-gold haze snakes down the culverts.
Summer fans like a deck of face cards, and closes--
a hot breath blowing into a cloud of cold hands. . .

Even if weather comes--split lip of thunder
shower, thick skirt off hurricane--the ground,
wind-thumbed and slick as board, will give up the
                                        dust
and no more to rain late and less than a blessing.

In our cities of Spanish Saints
flowers burn out with no compunction to return--
we take for granted the light at our fingers' ends,
the spread of dark growing between, and do not look
                                        up--
star cinders, vatic river we are floating out toward.

Fresno, 1976

Though the filtered daylight sifts down,
it is not the same--hard rains before picking
left growers shaking their heads
among a nation of ruined fruit. . .
Last visit, a moon ripe over vines of Chardonnay
and the heat loud on the whirring of insects.
Tonight, we sit out in long sleeves, jackets,
cheeks stung cold with the clear breath of stars
as the moon sinks into hurt orchards of Kadota
and currents burst like fists of blisters.
Jon and I share a blood-thick Pinot Noir, mute and
spell-caught by a ground-wind's elegy through leaves.

Morning, and a drive through country to the Kings
to praise life in the parables of river stone.
Childhood was the ritual tedium of relations
motoring through grey fields of Ohio,
but now there is nothing better than this
continuum of grasses, the blank paragraphs of hills.
Jon recalls that out this way, in the middle of
                              nothing,
is the sallow cemetery of first cow-men and settlers,
the plots drifting down a century to family.
We go there because those we read have gone,
because of the arcane inscriptions on stones,
because we would place our hands sideways in
                              wounds.
It's Veteran's Day and we hesitate
expecting mourners, but there are none--
two flags in cans stationed out for flowers
were ragged and flew only forty-eight stars.

On the far side, a gaunt Chicano boy digs
through a man's length of earth, and there is nothing
between markers spelling "BABY" or "unknown" but
                                        sun-
bleached plastic roses or gladiolas spinning in the
                                        cans,
and the thousand rivulets rain cut racing off the dirt.
One marker pointed an index finger skyward
saying, "Gone Home," and we looked up to what
we had seen before--the circumscribed and vacuous
                                        blue
and the uselessness of what we have to say
facing the steady dissolution of wind
which turns this hill to a canker
on the dumb tongue of the past.

*   *

Driving home, high winds on the heels of the cold
and the day begins to fail around 4:30--
the sky over Santa Ana smears
like a bloody thumbprint on glass,
a ruined rose of clouds. Down Interstate 5,
the unctuous breath of slaughter houses,
the babylonian walls of UniRoyal steaming away.
And looking back, even the pure water,
the clean air, left the fruit wasting.
We manage, labor, take up what we can, and finally
have only words for it at our fingers' end.

Soon, it's Friday and with the rest
I'm driving home at Five in long traffic;
far ahead, signals are mad stars over the intersection.
Boys in short-sleeves, salt-and-pepper corduroys.
are down dividers holding up carnations white and
                                        red,

almost saintly in tissue paper; they push them in
                              windows
as if they were not well dressed or living comfortably
near Newport Beach--they try the tired expressions
of the poor and I almost hear boys by churches
in Mexico City, "Flores, flores, flores para los
                                   muertos."

I try to ignore their saddened syntax of eyes
and the obvious perfidy of flowers--
I could give them to myself for times I've fumbled
my situations like change across a counter,
to the woman across the fence who never speaks,
to anyone for as long as they would last.
But the boys have been waving them for hours
and they're bending limp, heads bobbing in the dusk
as street lamps come on and mark where we've been
with the light dying early in December.

14 *VISITING*

for Steve and Francis

My hair fell out in Santa Barbara--Weldon Kees

September, when the silver trout slide
closer to the surface of the Santa Ynez,
the thin bones of my hands do the same. . .
I come back to what I have not outgrown,
breathe in and feel the city, wondrous,
in its advanced dream of plants.

And each time the ending swims before me
in intoxicant arms of sunlight,
the seduction of olive crowns to soil.
The eyeless wound of a pepper tree
shows how it will be when I no longer break
from sleep and ask the names of things;
how it will be when Sunday finds me
telling my prayers on wine-scented hibiscus,
pitching bocce-ball at Arnoldi's with paisans.

Along East Valley Road, the eucalyptus are bare,
trimmed smooth as a school girl's legs;
acacias sprinkle pollen the color of rain.
In my friend's yard, the loquats are ripe,
the leather-yellow skins thick about their seeds.
He comes home with a sack of beer for the porch--
we watch clouds puff over the Figueroa range
like the priest's housekeeper wringing out
the wet hems of her dresses.

Hitting 30, the talk and beers go more slowly;
foxtails are picked from habit and tossed down wind.
What there is to remember is all about us--
bruised light sinking on 6:00 hills,
Angelus rising from the church of Mt. Carmel;
and the ground loosening around our hearts
as we sit back and relax, half way there. . .

The sun starts over
the eastern wash
pink as oleander and
the dense horizon flares
like a smudge pot flame.

Frank would come in
from the orchards,
all night spent in smoke--
pitch covering face and clothes,
the acids of citrus and sweat.

He was a lawyer doing well
and could have hired it out.
But each time he dressed
his chaffed and frost-stung hands
he said, "What I've saved
is worth the trouble."

I would fix Ovaltine and the chill
would loosen from his bones.
In the dim kitchen his face
would glow as he spoke of the lemon.

It is December in Redlands.
Frank is gone now several years,
and I visit mother on holidays.
To comfort her, last night I went
beneath the winter sky lighting pots
among the few trees that remain.

Finished, I sat outside in my parka,
peeling an orange, huddled on myself
like a bear--Orion chasing into light,
the steam of my breath going up
with the smoke from oil.

Southern California, Spring / Summer 1976

I

These things placed me on the earth:
my mother's cries and the high forceps
bruising me into the light,
the beads around my left wrist clicking
the holy bracelet of my name.

I was raised on the emblems of the Faith:
grey souls in Limbo,
fires of Purgatory indelibly at our backs,
and we looked for anything to save us
from the nun's hickory switch.
Six years old and from the Stations of the Cross
I learned to say "ignominious," learned
the "Glory Be" and the bowed head.
Later, rings I wore, lapis, jasper, agate,
said back my name to me in small riches,
but never too sure in sleep, I wore the medals always...

II

That day in Laguna, when a pacific breaker
wrestled the St. Christopher from my neck
I came up from the white water nevertheless,
searched the shallows and backwash for hours
to show only a rind of salt beneath each brow,
the same scars from rocks I dashed my knees against.

In a tidepool I saw the lines beginning to show
in my face, the crows-feet gripping east / west.
Low gusts sang in some empty bottles

as I recounted each thing I held and fell asleep
naming stars and orange blossoms coming on.

III

East to the desert, sun swinging low over 111,
I turn off at Rancho Mirage and see
no one has bought the old place.
Beside the sun-broken drive, citrus sag with fruit
hard-dried as blood--beneath the tires
acacia leaves crush like paper lanterns.
In an irrigation lane my shadow slides over silt
as the first stars spray a nimbus of light--
all the eyes of family calling home.

Winds uncover abrasions in rock and
I hear childhood resonances of latin prayer,
rough bones the desert rattles in its spell--
white hosts of windchimes across back yards
reassuring us that someone is there--
beyond this I'm not certain what is left. . .

IV

Back roads through Riverside where
last April's fire took it down to nothing--
the only blossoms are white profusions
of cabbage moths flitting from stick to stick.
Passing the junk yards of Corona,
autos smashed and stacked like fishheads,
the tapping of the pushrods says
this one too is grinding down.

Heading north, the train yards of Rialto, Fontana--
Southern Pacific, Cotton Belt, Dixie, and Burlington

piled on the side tracks with their bloodsalt dusting.
Above the tracks groves of eucalyptus
shelter Painted Ladies fluttering up from Mexico;
the amber pollen of their wings prints leaves
before they blow loose in the wind from traffic.
When the boxcars stream down line by night,
wheels spin back the silver filament
from the yard lamps and a moon.

V

Outside Santa Barbara fog plods up foothills
with the sadness of each thing forgotten,
each thing grown and fending for itself--
the lemon bearing thorns to remind our fingers,
the orange burning naked into the teeth of winter,
the violet jacaranda flooding streets
in sorrow for the un-named who built
in beauty, in bone, in mission walls,
those who cannot sleep locked in the land's heart.

Ysidro, Ysidro, acolyte of this chapel of hills,
when silences bundled like sticks upon my back
you took my half-sleeping hand and wrote,
"Words like wild grass pushing against the sky,
fingers veining the lips of creeks, scattered
among oak leaves, anise stalks, and I wake up
                              singing."
Like the cactus apple, your heart holds spines.
I lit twelve candles to St. Francis of The Lost
to un-cuff you from this dream, from my hands
wringing the darkness for other eyes.
We must stop calling on the apostles of the rose,

there is no voice in the water of Seven Falls,
no white deer in the mountain creeks--
nothing is left for charm.
Stones, there are only stones,
and we must bear them out.

II HEARTLAND

6:00 and around the cul-de-sac
TVs throw a haze onto lawns;
a woman peeling onions looks out
then pulls the curtains closed.
Along the sidewalks school children
have dropped their papers--
glittered angels and the over-large words
are helpless on the wind.

A hummingbird circles the red hibiscus
wings keeping time with the sinking light.
I open the mailbox to no mail
and my finger tears on the rusted edge.
I hold it beneath the hose
and for an instant see tiers of votive candles,
flames fluttering, small wings shadowed from the
                                        glass;
my grandmother entering her church in Columbus
and lighting candles for the lost,
for souls in Purgatory and a partial indulgence,
for her stiff knees and irregular heart,
for the cold and for her husband
passing like smoke above her prayers. . .

I come-to watching the threads of blood
burn out in the water, the cut going
white as beeswax, the sky wick-black.

I
Arthritis swelled her knuckles like curdled milk
and doctors said Eva would never have a child.
But she linked together transparent beads
and prayers repeated off her fingers
until my father was the pure image
cut from the glass of Eva's heart.
Her life became a small globe spinning
in an infant's hand. Her husband, Lon,
was made to swear off drink and she left him
nights to complete her novenas, left him
with the late hours and the broken light
of a black and white TV.

There was snow seven months a year.
If anyone was ever cold, it was never mentioned--
no one needed to be held.
There were squirrels in the white oak trees,
an Oldsmobile in the garage, the shops of Columbus.

II
Aunt Valaska ran a beauty parlor in her basement
never finding herself beautiful enough to marry--
for all the years there was only Bernie
who came at night for beer. There was a weekend
at the lake that never amounted to anything more.
For a while she raised parakeets on the side--
one spoke to her in her own voice;
the rest chittered to themselves like ladies
beneath the great pink helmets in the basements.

Her backyard sloped below the house
and held the heavy rains in a single pool.
Crab apples stood out against the dull sky,
fell from the tree into the dull water,
ringed the edge, a line of red pearls.
When I'd visit, I'd stack the apples
along the top window in the attic room
and let them recall the sun.

III

I moved around on the west coast
with my father reminding me to write east
once a year. Sometimes he would telephone.
On winter mornings along the chilled sea
I'd pick up bits of sanded glass:
chips of beer bottle, brown as dried blood,
pieces opaque and white as flakes of snow.
When the sky seemed sewn to the water
I would hold a coffee cup like a shell
to my ear, hear nothing, and think of them.

IV

Eva calls long distance on social security checks;
85 and she has not felt well for 40 years.
My father tells her that she will outlive us all.
He tells her not to worry but it's no good
and she is calling too often. Eva would be loved now,
would have the emotion she controlled
like linking chain on rosary beads.

In a picture Eva sent, she and Valaska stand
in front of a double trailer home, their late 50s
fox stoles are snapped tooth to tail.

Lon is not walking well so he is not in the photo;
he doesn't come to the phone when Eva is calling.
She asks for any photo of myself in recent years,
but there is not one that would get through
to a small town near Chillicothe.

V

I think of them as a west coast fog
has kept things grey for days, Ohio grey--
grey as that river and as slow, even, and unexacting,
weighed down with everything poured into it.

And on days like this I see without any trouble:
Aunt Valaska's felt driving gloves,
Eva's garter stockings that run
into the high button shoes that Lon made,
the 50 years he cut and stitched
settled grey as dust in his eyes,
Eva's tarnished rosary chains that break
and let the smoothed beads through,
the icicles on the trailer awning until late April.

Clouds drift in a nondescript sky
and I see my father who is moving again
for all the good it will do.
The dimes drop and I hear him
ease away over the phone, grey and fading
as my face in the booth's silted glass.

for Cheryl

12 years away and you go back to it--
that proud and middling heart
pragmatic as rock
sieved through steel and stadiums,
the windflower way of a people
taken hold where they land forever.

You were thinking of crocheted quilts,
the doilies sewn around bottle caps,
and not the mill grist sinking
to your grandfather's insides
or choking up the river's craw.

Like a sudden gust that nudges
the tired-hard tongues of shoes
left on a porch, you go among
relatives, their very minds
drifting absently like dust
taken off high above the earth--
the incidental mote sifting down
to land on an iced tea or
pint of rye hidden in the garage.

A sliver of sunlight through the awning
brushes the hands of aunts who touch
about your cheeks with fingers
cold as dough and who whisper
of apricots, ripe persimmon moons.

At the table where your mother sat
pouring canned milk in coffee,

you count the coupons into piles
which discount your grandmother's
Postum, margarine, and salts--
the repeating list repeating years.

Up early on a drive to Akron or Warren.
You see them line up in a grey dawn
to take their places, stone-faced,
under the grinding wheel;
or filing off swing-shift
blank from the blast furnace,
take the concrete turnpike home
where someone irons or washes-out
the soiled cotton-twill, bakes Perohis
for the Christening or Engagement.

Each thing you've ever seen
you see one more time,
and you write that you marry lucky
from this place or die
out the back door,
and no life like this. . .

Kentucky, West Virginia, Spring '77

> *. . . as the*
> *fishes that are taken in an evil net, and as the birds that*
> *are caught in the snare; so are the sons of men snared in*
> *an evil time, when it falleth suddenly upon them.*
> *(Ecclesiastes IX, 12)*

Leaves shed before they turned,
miller moths hit about the screens,
a black snake lolled in a coffee tree,
horns of the moon pointed down.
By these signs grandfathers divined
a hard-bound rain, but it meant nothing
as shirt-sleeve days unstuck
the fat-thick winter freeze and all
at once the Big Sandy was under doors.
Waist-high or to the neck, towns
were gut-shot, fish in a barrel--
slugged in with a county of mud.
A silt that could raise the iced seed up,
add five hands to a field of wrapper-leaf
killed the by-standing store and truck-patch,
filled the pick-up's hood and the mouth
of a child's talking doll--men dug like dogs
to come up with their homeless bones
which could not be told one from another.
One more rain and Federal Relief machines
clear away; the river recedes. People
like the worn shoulders of limestone,
bear down, set-in and over their heads.

 BRANDENBURG, KENTUCKY
(after the tornado, Spring '74)
for Go

I

The house Grandmother was born in
stood in the blue grass that the wind bent
toward the river--I remember her dresses
full with flowers and blossoms of clouds.
One street ran up-hill from the river,
a Chevrolet garage at the top.
Everyone farmed but after the Second War
they couldn't keep all the children home.
Steam boats churned the muddy water white
and this river-front town was America
in her softest cotton dress.

II

My father moved us west
and we settled for Southern California.
Grandmother would write us without fail;
birthdays, holidays, she enclosed
pictures of snow, ice frozen
in stalks thick as fence posts.
She would say, "The blackberry vines
will soon be running. Do you remember
cutting biscuits with a water glass?"

Almost every man she knew made the ground
give with their roughened hands.
She saw her husband, father,
and oldest children die;

felt things run through her
in their own good time.

This Christmas I told her
that I was writing,
that my hands were soft as pillow slips.
I told her I was looking for voices
in the bronze throats of grain,
and I did not say
that everything is going fast, changing--
that here, the orange groves disappear,
and the sun goes down in thick air
like a flower on a Hawaiian shirt.

I did not tell her that I'm afraid,
afraid that when I find a voice,
what I love will be gone. Grandmother,
the land will fold like newspaper
and there will be nowhere to return.

III

In March and April sodden winds pick up,
seed with electricity, dark sparks of pollen.
Last week they blew from all points
of the sky, formed a funnel
and cut a swatch down Tornado Alley.
Twisters tore up roots of buildings, fences,
tore them like straw and left the land
opened for miles around.

Water fell like rocks from the black tube.
A leg of the radio tower
sprung easily as a paper clip,

clerks crouched in the Courthouse vault.
A length of iron pipe drove clean
through the neck of a cow.

Grandmother was in the basement
when her roof lifted and spun away.
Her porcelain animals lay in pieces
on their sides, a dry flower had split
the mirror. She began to sweep up
and then just leaned against a wall,
eyes clouding grey with water.

IV

Phone lines were tied up for hours.
When I got through there was only
the dead humming of wire--
she had left for Lexington,
almost everyone had gone.
On the roadsides,
roots of the great cedar trees
tangled in the air. As easily as dandelions,
the white boards of the houses had blown away,
the last screen door swinging open.

V

A letter arrives from Lexington.
There are only a few sentences
spread around the paper.
I touch the white spaces, spaces white
as flour that will not dust from fingers.
Grandmother sends along a picture
to show she is all right.

In it I see my hands in her hands,
the deep channels of her brow continuing in mine.
Her dress is brocaded brown and mauve with iris--
I see the river slow and darken
in the stems without roots,
the land dissolving, and our lives running out.

A fan rotates on the screened porch,
on the divan great grandfather nods
into the bib of his overalls.
Beneath the shade trees they sit
on white metal lawn furniture--
grandmother in a cotton dress
pink with camellias, pours iced tea;
grandfather in sleeveless undershirt
puts a transparent handkerchief to his face
and dabs at the sweat.
Mother brings out the portable RCA
and tunes in the local station--
a car whines down Route 60 toward Louisville,
the music lilts and she sings along
in a voice thin as the heat waves
rising from the road.

From behind the house a boy runs out,
his finger red as Kool-Aid stains on his shirt.
Grandfather rides him on his knee
and ties a handkerchief tight to the cut. . .

A few years later he will carry dinner
to his grandfather's bed, hear him call out,
"A man can't be expected to live
on these thimble-sized biscuits."
And he will run to the kitchen
where the women are saying nothing.

But now, he sits a minute and stares into the radio.
Aunt Tade picks up her straw fan and begins,

a peacock in deep blues unfolds on one side--
there is speculation about who will come visiting
and the chairs cricket as they watch the shade
advance the afternoon and surround the house.

for Aunt Shelly

There is a time in the year for us--
we come to life under a hard star,
come to trouble in a blood-thin month.

Daylight soaked in a shawl of mist,
feeling gone from hands, color from leaves,
and in your yard the roots of maple trees

made fists beneath ground bone-sore with ice--
raspberry briars thinned up the house side
like blood vessels broken in a cheek.

You watched for nothing through the window,
thought of your daughter and counted
the indifferent rabbits slipping across snow.

Your love went out to the cherry sapling
staked and bound with the sash of your dress,
its few boughs shaking like your will.

There was the last day and a dark rain
blowing with the months of uneven sleep,
your waist gone to a girl's from worry.

Cold face to face, the lives kiss-out,
and we tell sorrows down the train-years,
love with some photographs losing light.

Bitter herbs break the earth of our enduring
and there is the heart that actually bursts
and leaves us holding our own. . .

Which of us can really say
what we could have been
beyond the love of love or labor
we gave ourselves away to,
slim in some photographs
of our all-fired youth?

Now a skin of circumstances
has grown past all that;
the gold band
tightens to the bone
and cuts a little feeling off
like some blue-note roadhouse
saxophone fading out the 40s.

You sang your sister's
harmonies, church or swing,
until she took her chances
on a radio man moving west. . .
the hotels of Louisville
in a silver mesh of light
where you-all all night danced
up a red-eyed dawn.

Your daddy's farm is parceled, half gone.
The celestial boards of the big house
face-lifted by brick to push
spinning wheels and hand-crank phones,
varnished relics that now cure nothing.
The catfish ponds are parched
to standing water no deeper
than the tracks of tires.

When you drive west past Louisville
you take the highway on complaint--
the hotels slouched and brackish,
the streets hard to see down
as the river they edge.
You can't remember where the main ones
might have led--someone
with half a story
on the back of their tongue.

You steam hours away ironing
shirts--clothes drop down
the chute to cellar or in the hall,
and you cook the day in shifts.
You put the netted suet out
to keep jays and cardinals
through the snow-high months;
midday, squirrels tightrope
the yard on phone lines
to also get it; no cheeped
invectives as you've set out enough.
And the household's home for supper--
the daily blessing and song
of those who expect of you.

When you do sit down with coffee,
what never occurs is what it was
you wanted some time ago in sepia.
You go back. The iron presses
the afternoon into five creases.
You recall the horse tethered in circles
at the sorghum mill, and somehow
how the long miles turn it sweet...

You do not have time to think
if time has proved love to be all
it was talked-up to be; sun breaks early
in a window and the husband bolts
from bed and talk slips off with sleep.
But each winter you see the mimosa leaves
wrinkle and line-out below life,
and hold your hands up to your face.
You see the cranes drifting south in Fall,
the men going off to jobs
no longer bound to love the land.

But you do not worry what runs-out;
you get them through their days.
By evening on a songless rest
small flames skip within your eyes--
gone windowgrey they reflect
a heart that's grained a way
above it all. Who would come to love
if everyone took off to dance and sing?

for James Riley Miller

From bluegrass to Appalachia they still mark
Old Christmas by Julian Calendar and say
at midnight the barnyard has the gift of speech;
sheep and cattle kneel in tongues, stars chorus.
They hold the abiding life in soil,
believe each winter-broken seed pulls up
with light. They pray one vow of color--
green/yellow of corn, of bean, and tobacco;
green/yellow of John Deere tractors
which parse and verse the fields.
They stay thick-blooded in the long cold,
in what they recall and look forward on.

Grandmother traces us firmly back
five generations to French Miller and beyond
to a tin-type of a woman whose name is dust
but who was our first breath before us.
She tells grandfather's belly rippled, gangrened
past complaint, luck of a neighbor's Ford
that got him to Louisville where
they cut a burst appendix out; tells how close
it was, early, before my mother was born.
More daguerreotypes and tea-colored prints--
one of farm hands standing together, the color
of earth the color of their skin, showing
how they'd taken to it--beneath crumpled hats
their faces lean into a line of sunflowers.
We see others stiff in collars and high-backed chairs;
handed down, the invisible margins of this life.

*   *

What I see clearly is grandfather's 20 gauge
knocking crows from above the corn
right as sunlight; 4 years old, the ordination
of buckshot showing the way on a man's own land--
feathers falling where they may. Evenings coasting
on the back porch glider, he'd spit *DaysWork*
and admire "see-peeps" croaking from the cistern,
and late he'd walk out near a shade tree
in the front and piss beneath the stars.

*   *

Still, his farm is partly there
lonesome with a few cows and blasted trees.
I visit the cemetery hard-found beneath weeks
of snow and the tornado of three years past--
elms spun clean away, stones windslammed.
At our plot I do not want to think about my life--
brown pelican in a slick Pacific--
or think of Baptists' gut-tight grip,
or cities and what they never mind.
I want to do the little that I can
which will not matter either way, but should--
wholly say some thanks for someone simply good,
read his three names aloud and leave
the long drawn vowels like lovesongs on the land.

For a month now it's humid as the mid-east,
and the sky, thick as if sifted with flour,
has the faint rose of gasoline.

This is Irvine, almost the last land
to go in southern California--
next to a new tract, a few swaggering trails
and cows trundling out; haydust and dung mix
on the air over University Boulevard.

*   *

Law school by mail and James Miller
was the last man electioneering on horse;
farms spread over Mead County, Kentucky,
like something the wind blew,
and he rode them down,
talked the Brandenburg gasbags
and the black folks of Frogtown.

Fifteen years for the County, Clerk and Judge,
then he retired to his land
with his last two-toned Chevrolet Belair.

*   *

I rode the tractor and combine,
watched the fields pour wheat and the hay bale,
lugged peach baskets of string beans
from Go's acre garden.

But the country went sour in its gut;
they couldn't raise or plow under enough.
Uncle Codge went back to Olin Mathieson,
chemical vats which spotted his blood
and left Bessie listening to company doctors,
small print, and not a dollar from the policy.

*   *

Sundays I went visiting with the women.
We left Daddy-Jim off halfway to nowhere
at country stores with boards in the windows
and old men on the benches; they called him "Judge"
and chewed all day--the jawsmiths of Wolf Creek.
I remember his high purple socks, calf-tone shoes,
how above me faces of the men
were the weather-eaten water towers
our train passed on the way back west.
I recall his face smooth as a silver dollar
from straight razor and strap,
the handkerchief dabbing his blue-grey eyes
as he waved from the platform in Louisville--
hell was somewhere west of the Mississippi
and he was sure it was slipping east. . .

*   *

I haven't been there in ten Decembers
except in the repetition of a dream. . .
fields blank as the eye of a crow
and on the rise where the red barn
kept cattle and cured tobacco,
a stucco house and nylon patio chairs.

I walk into the white slat farmhouse
where no one comes from the cellar with preserves
or scolds about weak brick around the cistern,
where I cannot find the chipped teeth
of an upright piano or a boy unfolding fingers
to the pulse of a lightning bug.

I am alone, half-lost in history,
listening for Go in the morning dark,
the snap of her match and cough of the stove. . .
I come back to myself,
wakened by cars in my complex,
and realize there's nothing to be done,
nothing dreams can fix
in the face of engines warming up
and their people going off
to work for our great industrial trusts.

III CORRESPONDENCES

for Robert Lowell

Christ! What will we look to now,
those of us who didn't even know
they called you "Cal,"
those many of us coming after
like unleashed hounds on scent?
(Do we dig up a moss-green El on Third
or take a drive down Stuyvesant?)
We have hardly any years
that do not resonate with you,
and though it seemed each one
showered on some dope or screw,
you, you were coming in
from the stiff of things
and sounding-out your life.

The saying crossed your heart
but you muscled through
bound letter-tight to each
blue circumstance that came apart.
Adumbrated, we looked for Fall
and took to schools with beer and
books in cases that hurt our heads.
But on some shore, or in bed,
I turned your pages week to week,
couplets biting like beach-
spray on my cheeks--a couple years
we studied not so much
our lives as yours.
And before we wrote or thought

to write, lines bear-like
chased up our spines
and bore home your anviled
leagues of Latinate. It seemed
the meat and sawbones of our speech
were not all ours at all.
We can look to stars, the gleam
where we are cast and figured in
the wheel, and feel the spokes
touch us where we're sore.

We watched for everything you said
except that last line
failing through your chest . . . .
Our hearts are not so large
that we can wholly take you in.
At the very least we hoped
you did not despair to see
the plain sad axis on which we spin.
Let the words you found
in Santayana's mouth be at last in ours,
"There is no God
and Mary is his Mother."

What is beyond this you are not sure, and
regardless, to focus past this crush of sky
avoids the end-line and cast-lot a life comes to.
So you let the blue be blue, day-down and sunk blue--
just as well a sea out there sucking at us
as this sky, the land falling off to it
flat on a grating drone. This splay shock
of grain holds the light apart from any use,
holds it in armfuls to an indifferent wind;
you say we are essentially dirt-lonely.

Something slips off the squid-bleak borders
breath-thin--clouds that are seen through
shaping nothing, the iced petal of the iris,
the vague light let out the bitten finger's end
dull as the straight razor barely looking back
beneath old water in the basin, scudded-over
as the mildewed walls of institutions where
like beds, lives even out beyond their breadth.
And desires wear down with faces on the coins
once kept in your good pocket for luck,
that luck cracked in china cups
of eyes that now refuse all light but this.

Your week's sorrel growth of beard corresponds
to this burnt-red road; its valve-like split
could stand for the heart if there were feeling
of one left anywhere, so much as a stone
we could conjecture to a heart's residue,
a wood-dry pit of the thing; but nothing.
And we do not see the way out offered

in this split through the flow of wheat.
This then is how we argue with ourselves,
come to be of three minds until it's no use.
and we come unchanneled like a river's end.
The letters slip back into ink and muddy-out
the memory until a brother is a blond oak chair
in a tilted room and stars are something else again--
the last things you touched gone in a blaze.
And we do not wonder if rain will come or stars
or anything after these days. We feel
pieces of us flying off like bits of rag,
crows darting in the warp of wind and elements,
the last down beating of the wings before
that sure fall into this very air.

for Sherod Santos

There are stars, thrown
like a net over each thing you said,
but none shine here.
It is pitch deep as a cave,
a darkness pressed onto the air;
your eyes are closed because
you know what figures bray about you.

The only light is the torch
in a beefy pirate's hand,
yet you see the star you were born beneath,
the kiss, and the one word
you are taken with.
The green mantle of the pharisee
does not conceal his envy
or hawk-like bead on your blood--
goat-eyed glance, apish hunker in a brow:
they know what they are doing.

Simon's knife preys down an ear,
the others are just coming-to--
hands at your throat, yoked
like a horse, you pulled these
second-guessing souls along, but
now you will wait them out.
When this sky goes sallow and grey,
Gethsemane's far leaves fade
with any promise you can recall,
there will be one more thief
to whistle at your heart for heaven
before you are released.

What is clear at first is that
your bed narrows to a ledge,
a slab you barely fit;
a boulder no sun has softened
is offered in the way of a pillow.
But at 23, almost everything fits
or soon will--half-moon of tracks
in the stone around the hearth
left by the old ones who shuffled off
with their sacred names
but not their shoes; the discomfort
from their lives handed down
so regular and dull, it often sleeps.

What we cannot avoid are your hands
the size of goatskulls, thick mules
that could beat a man down,
leather straps that break loose
parsnip, potato, and beet, roots and all--
hands that grip the big iron spoon
and pound the lentils into soup.
And your waist lean as a meat knife
means you eat from habit,
that the greaseless flesh of plants
is not enough to satisfy.

What these grey sands of eyes imply
so do half-seen pictures on the wall,
there is little to remember--
windows blank on shirt-tails of fog,
the water-logged skin of your land.

Ice-skinned poplars pin-stripe a distance
wool-heavy as a convict's sleeves,
perhaps the origin of the shirt you wear.
One apple tree is wind-tangled, sprung
as the one side of your chestnut hair.

But finally we have it in the face--
the flared and drawn lines of cheek
the earth pulls at each day
with the weight of the cold.
The final and almost full turn of jaw,
stubborn to be young and at this,
tells us what passes in a life
much more than strings of smoke
from slate chimneys, blowing
with the silver hair of the old into nothing.

You conceded some rouge to just the mouth--
lips vibrant as a cat, a color suggesting
you have the heart for it if the way was clear
to this flame-eyed and fire-handed man.
He says you are the first, all the others
will come after you; his eyes will now always
break around a face the way this long light
sees down yours and reduces this horizon;
the way you carry in your bones the sinking
of unmeasured fear for unmeasured work,
the bound breasts of undetermined love.

The men are off with their heavy animals
and you are out and back on the daylight
to the fields--you do not let yourself think
of them or one who turned to you often

during the month of onions, who never knew
you looked back. And months have built in you
like stone flecks from mill wheat adding
to a rock's weight which drops down burning
where it must--and soon, after 25,
the blood which flushes in one cheek
will blanch and years will be hard things
pushing their way through, hard things to take--
the beefy embrace, the tongue going to clay
to just keep warm and indoors late winter.
It will be harder to look back at this
or any other painting which repeats
your face a hundred ways in thinning,
repeats the life that sold you out by degrees,
but kept your silhouette and that one shade of red,
the uncompromised blood that stones absorb.

Peter--another summer closes and on what? One
more slab of work wedged free like block ice? We
manage place to place and part way, uncertain when
to pack it in or begin again. With weather on the
way, I've been thinking of you--snow, and you'll be
out of work with the season. I've done with a second
summer session, broken the light of language into
lumps, principles of composition, wondering what
part-time will be handed out for Fall. I feel we are
coming to something, almost there: frozen trail break-
ing up, but it hasn't yet ground down to easy going--
one place we can stake-out and catch three breaths
in peace. No one believes you until you're 40, thick-
skinned as a bear, fingers so tight at the throat of
what you want, that loosening them, you find you
half killed the thing you first took hold of. You must
be musing on the park's avalanche of clouds stepping
off distance the way ice floes take a river on, or watch-
ing winds hard at the tops of trees, the year-round
sourdoughs slapping up storm doors and windows be-
fore the first ice flying down like fighter planes. . . I
wonder if you still dream them streaming over Indo-
China, night-fire, tracers, dying through a quick burn
of woods? You got through it, and it got you this job
in the half-wilderness with your half-year house on
the water where you stare evenings up into the stilled
sky's thought. If you pick up an off-season stint,
you'll comb the Santa Barbara Islands' salted bones or
find yourself polite at Pt. Reyes with tours. This old
worry of vocation, what we gave up imagined big
money for, is a slight numbness in the knee, old war
wound, pain that says we're still here for something,

with a medal, but somehow at a loss. Winter will
find us anywhere but where we most remember--
church-still foothills in Montecito, the outposts of
pepper trees and avocado. There was snow there only
once, '54 I think, but all the same, it was a feeling
kept us running chill mornings red-cheeked in the
fog-bound air. Do you remember music lessons drum-
med out by thick-skinned Sisters of The Immaculate
Heart? The *dal segno* directing us to return and repeat
from the sign? Now, with each coda in the weather,
we turn and mark where we last began. . .blue cords,
ocean-checked shirts--parochial uniforms from grade
2 up. We were the last with baseball cards, and this
time of year we were hounding nuns for The Series
during class, tuning-in a snowy black-and-white TV.
These images nicely lack contrast or definition, string
us along through 30, help us see this life forward over
that common ground where we booted the ball. And
not long ago, I was playing doubles at noon with
Oakley Hall and the professors on the campus courts,
the wisteria in lobs over the April fence like pleasant
dreams. But yesterday, on the abandoned schoolyard,
I saw poor Italians picking summer's last wild olives.
Dark eyes of a father looked down from his ladder as
if to say, "Take what you can and what else?" I
thought of us getting by, occasionally where we want
to be, but still holding out for livelihoods to fill--we
quit smoking and cut hard drinks almost altogether,
and I know sometimes nervously we look at our hands
to see what we have left. And so for these good
reasons, I enclose a small postcard of a Pieter Brueghel.

The print is a detail from "Winter Landscape."
All work is stopped here, but we can surmise some
months of strict repetition in the fields, meditation of
hands on hoes. Hay colored bricks send a gold sheen
across the ice where children spin their tops from
sticks, and young men are curling stones. The women
must be inside, houses dear with warm baking air.
The boat for rowing up river to store is sleep-full of
snow; no one fishes through the ice, the birds sit fat
and careless, the faint cross of a windmill is stilled
in a bright vanishing of hills. Notice the two men
in long coats content to look on--they take it all in,
as long as the heart thaws; they have come to feel
just like themselves with or without the work, hav-
ing adjusted to the cold--

        be seeing you,

for Jon Veinberg

Again light sinks earlier
and dust builds like bags under eyes.
I have a fire in the hibachi
and no one to call over for a drink.
There's little to point to
this fall--bare sycamores turning
to bad handwriting on the distance.
banana tree and no flesh-red flower.
Only the astringent persimmon
bears-out this time of year
hot-orange as the coals;
the smoke lifts and thins
with half the things I remember.
At this time of day I know
you're watering that army of roses,
sack of beer under your left arm,
the pose of a running-back, though
you say you intend to take it slow.
I'm watching the olive leaves
take up the silver-blue from water
and reading over magazines and mail.
They're still writing about fathers--
the boot grinding in from the 2nd War,
absences deeper than the obvious
light-years of death.
Death or love, they left,
or were never there at the start--
you were born running mid-ocean
to the sore arms of women and broken English;

memories of Russians on loudspeakers
and a father would be things you learned.
But we're tired of hearing how we grew
with so little to praise.
The letters are better--perhaps like prayer
no news on a familiar line, soothes.
Though, when the night comes clear,
you can't miss the syllabus of stars
pressing sharp as thorns
even your careful hands will not avoid.
So what are our points of reference?
Beer, flowers, the lost
faces of fathers in a cloud?
The rabbit-blood in days
does not let us catch breath
and even things out. The Faith was lost
some time ago, but the holy cards, the parables,
outlived the war of childhood,
like shrapnel or tattoos, the stories
recite inside our skin. And I see
Simon the Cyrenian saying nothing
as he takes up an end of the cross,
unsure what he's sharing in,
just doing what he learns by heart.

(Last note of a composition teacher)

My dearest Claire,

This life is like nothing
I ever planned or read about--
week to week and hand to mouth
I spooned the gravel of this language
onto slow tongues of the careless,
found myself reduced by time-sheets
and 1-5 evaluations of my style.
Each form was an x-ray
I could not interpret; I only felt
the vagueness coming over me,
which, if I had thought of it,
would have told me these days
were adding to a dark sum,
the blotting-out of cells
where what you were accrues.
And if I ever planned, I did so
as a man treading water--
the compulsive flutter of his feet
recalled only at last, in fear.
Each hour was incoherent, clotted
with dish-like faces of the young
who arrived in mid-sized cars
named for foreign principalities.

The instant coffee at 6:00
was only one of many things
forced down at an ungodly time.

Through a fabric of exhaust
each sun came up acetylene;
to hear the ring-neck dove resting
in her syllables was a suffering.
And I saw no warning signs
on the ash-grey walls of the academy
until one morning the absence of
anything went sour in my gut.
Home, I took the half-ripe oranges
from the neighbor's tree, made juice
and drank--acid bit the corners
of my mouth like a bad kiss.
What there is left I leave to you
with the remaining juice in the mason jar
because the check was small again this month.

Driving out, I seemed to remember
the smallest hours of relief
when sex wheeled us down to sleep
and the dour and phosphorescent
light of rooms sank with infinite
particles of our skin into the bed.
But love has little to do with it;
it is irrelevant to the pain.
And what do I deserve having bled
the pure words of my beginnings
into the moral turpitude
of 500 word themes? We paraphrased
the constellations to a scar.

As for children, we don't have any. . .
and I hope you can forgive

remarks about your mother
while talking in my sleep--
I wrote nothing down, so there's no way
to tell what I really felt.
I could not find time to prune
the frost-bitten pomegranate--
the dead-hard husks cluster and
still come at me in dreams, nodding
like heads along a row of desks.

I'm worn as the bent valves
of my japanese wagon--endings
of nerves and what they held together
are dulled from all the miles,
commuted or otherwise, as surely as
flesh struck in the same spot each day.
But this is Nebraska and it ends for now,
the long drive over the edge
to where the decay can be got at.
I think I have found the snow,
that worst of all winters
we read about in the *Times*.
The horizon here is blank and calm
as a fresh bandage--flakes of snow
are only flakes of snow and spell nothing.

Today, you would see postcards of royal palms sway,
banana palms roll gold as cigars in Beverly Hills.
January, and we are tanning in our shirt sleeves;
the sailboats flock like pigeons off Marina del Rey.
Even the poor rowing skiffs in Echo Park can turn
and see the modest snow peaked on close resorts.
You would say we have the best of both worlds
as if there were only two sides to this life,
as if there were not questions to be asked.
But off 101 the Castle Argyle and Hollywood Tower
are slack under their last whitewash, and dreaming--
they forget themselves like an aging actress, over-
powdered and spreading in an afternoon swoon of
                                        martinis.
The yellow grease of 50 years dims the windows and
                                        poses:
Who can live on the inconstant light of stars?

And though this winter of even heat fooled blossoms
and brought the tourist trade, it took our rain away--
it's all you can do to get a glass of water in a cafe,
all you can do to ignore the rank signs in a dire year.
The West died long ago, collapsed like a lung when
the gold bled out; bankers pumped in iron and rivers
and lettuce shined like coins; the oil produced two
                                        wars.
And now the hot Santa Ana winds have the call of
                                        creditors.

Our Utilities study the upper desert floor.
They puzzle at half this state's over-bite on the other,

at the salt-steam thrust they might harness from
a 10 mile bulge in the crust near Palmdale--better
they study the sand-white lizard slipping through
the bones of a horse, the asters pushing out the eyes.
We have built on a primary split down a length of
                                        land
like the line in your hand saying when your life will
                                        end.
The Indians on this western shelf said the quaking
was the dead fighting among themselves and that will
finally mean as much to us as anything. This
                              Evening
private planes sparkle with the spray of Christmas
                                    lights;
screen doors swing open to cool. The air is dry,
still as paint or unread roman numerals in the stars.
East and West, we hold down equal portions of this
                                        earth
against the steady suck of space--the imponderable
weight of nothing that pulls our atmospheres apart--
but we have all the people, the slippage of the plates
heading our way and down, and no reason to take
                                        heart.

for Danielle

This fall the frost snapped early
and for your fourth year
the almond flowers will not be back
nor the starlings who built nests.
Even if I were with you
I'm not sure I could explain.
It is like the day
a bird came in the open window;
I put him in your hands
and for a moment he did not stir.

Here, the leaves slide up the wind. . .
Sister Caritas prepared me for 1st Communion,
the Host would bleed if bitten or touched--
it was thin as a leaf or flower
pressed dry in an almanac.
I was 16 when a blade of grass fluttered
along my forearm, then a girl's finger. . .
Whatever we take to heart
slips sharp and neat beneath the ribs--
your mother put her fingers inside my chest
and shook me out like a dry sack of leaves.

The cottonwoods are a bare twist of branches.
A bruise-red leaf of the Chinese maple
blows over my shoulder--the wind swirls
small tides of dust, and this is as much
embrace as words will make.

 SAN CRISTOBAL DE LAS CASAS, Chiapas, Mexico

on the photograph by Lin Romero

It has been some time
since they reapportioned saints--
this child of ten despairs
knows nothing of that
or eternal Rome where they cut
St. Christopher adrift.
She knows lime and sandstone
houses once held on hope
in his mis-blessed name
and weathered chubascos busting
loose from Golfo Tehuantepec.
Centuries of amulets and
holy mentions, some safety
from the hundred hazards
and hurt ends in a road
are now so many wings torn
from bees in a wind storm.

The walls rain dust, cough chalk,
a thousand minute shells
blowing nowhere with the sand.
He shouldered children over
a river's swollen heart,
through small or chicken pox,
with the medallions scarred
across their living skin;
and for a while he held off
the blank clouds of poverty

from entering their eyes--
bore the world's weight
and held each beam in place.

But now her eyes lift
to where the dust drifts off;
it's as good a place as any
to find relief. A small mirror
aimlessly in one hand,
she is tired of what it reflects--
the other bunches back
her crow-black hair in the ancient
attitude of last questions,
"What becomes of it all?"
A dog watches with her.
Stone-white flames of eyes,
twin streaks below the chest,
recall totems of the Mayas--
their gods must have also aged
and likewise left them
with the stopped tongues of relics.
What of a patron who had
a staff, and a back of muscles
coiled like mountains,
now a shadow chased around
the fallen corner of home?
Faith dies in a slight
remembrance, an image
in someone's forgotten name,
prayers repeated into clouds.
Something in this photograph

and the dog that licks and guards
by this child's bare feet,
will save her before the medal
hung for years around my neck.

IV   LAST RITES

We will see more passing than any,
carry our fathers' grief
through three cultures.
And he tells me how that time,
highschool to the after-war-years,
runs together like a suit of cards,
Hearts let's say,
with Big Bands, the Big Beat, and Swing. . .
Before the war, after the war,
Saturday afternoons in New Jersey,
a swaying crowd of 10,000
at Frank Daily's Meadowbrook,
the sounds of Glen Miller, Claude Thornhill.

During the war, an airbase in Abadan, Iran--
the one disc of Vaughn Monroe worn to static,
once a month culling the frazzled air
for the British Broadcast--
Tommy Dorsey's slide trombone pure
as moisture steaming off a mirror
in the 120 degree shade, Sinatra & The Pied Pipers
with ''Blue Evening'' and ''Once In A While.''
Sundays, he'd skin the Persian Gulf in an A-20,
buzz a down-beat through
the anchored Russian fleet.

By the time I was three
I knew how to stand at the plate,
had seen Red Schoendienst turn the double-play,
and heard Julie London's foggy voice.
Now, hair dull as a Mercury dime,

he tells me I'm lucky
to be 30 and unmarried, meaning
the world lost heart by the 50s--
each man home, bent beneath a shoulder's weight
of family and got serious with dollars;
some devil split an atom
under a football stadium
and there was nothing
you couldn't care about.

He looks to me with the obvious,
"How time flies" or "Where do the years go?"
and examines his hands, fingers spread apart
as if he just made a deck of cards disappear
and can't remember how he did the trick.
He doesn't flip to the game of the week
or the up-dated weekend news, rather,
he stacks albums on the Magnavox--
the re-released recordings of an era
when life was coming to only moderate harm.

No aspirin and the instant coffee's gone,
red fish are swimming in my eyes.
I manage the safety razor high as the mirror
before I know to put it back.

On mornings-after I am always contrite.
And when I promise myself *never again*,
I remember the time Father Salvador caught us
drinking altar wine in the sacristy
and I promised to quit for good.
My mother warned and continues to this day:
"You'll walk a dotted line, one eye open,
both of your fingertips to your nose
and never say the alphabet complete."

Clouds hold to the edges of a tin sky
like bubbles in a stale glass of water;
the air is thick and damp as a towel.
Phone wires stitch across the window;
I watch the kite caught there for months--
its stick-man frame held together by string,
its tail limp as an amputee's sleeve.

This is the earthquake weather
my mother could feel in her bones--
a day of light wind, the imperfect sorrow,
that will shake it all down.

So often as we prayed
we grew used to our prayers--
Sisters of the Immaculate Heart
declared each one was heard and
we were given what was needed.

And it was nothing
to see the Mexican kids
counting holy cards
with a meatless lunch;
smiling Luis whispering
"Bless me ultima mariposa!"
into a brown crumpled bag.
On holidays, among eight
sisters of thin arms,
Amalia saying grace
over the baked sheep head--
". . . and these thy gifts
which we are about to receive
from thy bounty. . ."
relishing the soft grapes of eyes,
the chalky wedge of tongue;
ninos at the cheek bones for guns.

We learned the communion host
was body and blood in our mouths,
only the accidents
of bread and wine remained;
we learned not to chew
but take it in without question
like Latin and Gregorian Chant.

*　　*

Inching home in traffic,
air runs with the rust
of everything we've accepted,
and not a consonant of wind
off the ocean or from cars
the other way.
　　　　　Through it all,
the San Gabriel mountains
fade like calendar pictures
of the Holy Family
in the panaderias of east L.A.
My new used car has only AM
and stations play old songs,
give us clues to recall the times,
as if we could forget
the catechism that gave us
this day, this freeway south
we take on faith brings us
to our livelihood and back,
the hen's teeth of our desire,
my rosary of fourteen keys
opening the deaf stations
of someone else's dreams.

for Sozzi, Santa Barbara

The mock-adobe church of Mt. Carmel
murmurs in its weekday sleep--
Quadragesima Sunday, High Mass.
The faded purple cloth on saints
and wooden clappers in the bells;
the dampness and stale incense lilt. . .
I hear Sister Vincent de Paul
leading us in prayer, admonishing,
"Penance keeps the soul
white as a bottle of milk."

Down the flagstone steps children
still practice for May Procession;
girls are dropping invisible petals
around the statue of The Sacred Heart.
I see our initials in long white scars
on leaves of the sword-bill cactus.

We gave up the faith and fell away--
the town continued in Hispanic style;
the sandstone walls ran on to spite us.
The lace-like shade of pimiento trees
still meets in the middle of this
foothill road, but Peter, we go nowhere
if we are always coming back.

Shadows from the eucalyptus leaves
blow like ash across my forehead,
the lunch tables are empty
and swept with dusk.

Wind from a passing car
bends the yellow flowers of sourgrass--
the random patches of remembrance
that recall our sun-gone goodbyes.

for Frank

The rain all night,
a moth circling the study lamp,
wing dust rising
in a thin white smoke.

The priest returns--
oil in olive crosses on your skin,
your skin gone white to yellow
as the bread and lemon
used to cleanse his hands.

The Agnus Dei, a small silver bell,
and looking through the window
perhaps the last things you saw
were the street lamps swelling
into light like flowers.

*   *

It is seven years to the day,
early May, and even so
the air is cold as nails.
Only one road to the beach,
the cemetery on the edge,
and so I must drive by.
I have wondered what they think,
the people who visit--
there is nothing here
but the bouquets they leave
going to husks in the wind,

no mercy salted on the air:
who among us is ever ready?

Always it was right between us
so I need not come in
and recall before cold slates,
anoint this windowbox of absence.

I pull over down the road,
light a cigarette,
and watch the sun
burn through the fog,
a single white camellia.

for my stepsister

I

Nuns warbled their warnings
about the Mystical Body,
how one original sin would stain
the whole of us. . .
                    I day-dreamed
through the window and the chalk dust
watching for your horse-gold hair,
waiting out the bell.

There were pomegranates
growing behind the pool,
and I remember
thumbing purple seeds from the core,
the race, the bloodied knee.

II

When your husband threw his last glass,
beat you and left,
you just sat and watched
the mariposas rub against the screen. . .
I held you for all the wounds--
the stretch marks down your stomach
like a river where the mouth empties out.
I watched you sleeping
silver in the half-light of the mirror.

III

The morning climbs up 101,
you drive and we do not speak.

Outside Santa Barbara we pass fields
studded with purple thistle, a sail of mustard
blows in the vacant procession of hills,
off Point Rincon winter swells break
and flatten on the sand. . .

Your tightened jaw could be from cramps--
you once said you can feel the moon tug,
your blood sway like a minus-tide.
Your knuckles beading white on the wheel
say there is something in you
that wants to be through with it.

IV
People take on lovers like new skin.
It all turned out in the cards,
your second man on his head in my hand,
and there you read the deep and failing lines.

A child, you wanted to be a nun--
you thought of Bernadette at Lourdes
digging until her fingers bled and the water came.
You grew roses in the rocky strip by the garage,
made the garden come on through winter.
Now the grass is going brown, the mariposa to straw--
the light blue of your eyes goes grey
as your lovers breathing over you,
the faces all much the same.
And when you look for my face you find it
in the only photograph, taken in the snow,
and blurred beyond a trace.

V
In your sculpture, the dove dives
with a host into the cup--
the small blades of your shoulders
opened as perfectly. . .
and now in nights of drunkenness
the wings spread like a Harpy's
and beat above my head.

Winter's last rain has fallen. In the foothills
around MaryMount, the Angelus rings to no one,
no one in the courtyard bends to their knee.
The nuns are gone, the crows move in,
I wander through the abandoned school,
pick yellow sourgrass and chew the stems
knowing how you will be alone;
some water trickles down a window pane
and disappears into a stone.
As I light a cigarette against the wind
my hands assume the attitudes of prayer--
eyes on the white face of a midday moon
I ask for something like another day
and what goes up in the smoke
is the dark flower from my heart,
the bruise growing inward.

for Douglas

I wake to three ringings of the phone
and answer--"It's Sunday, 6:00,
and the sun is gone like a nickel dropped
through a glass of tap water."
Again, you're sitting on your patio, drinking,
missing even the most obvious stars.
You're thinking of women we've both lost,
of love so desperate it tightened
like a chloroformed scarf around their throats.
By now, there should be a specific complaint,
but what sinks in us is indistinct
as a clot of blood lost in an artery for years.

You say you have looked at the moon
and thrown up your hands for the last time;
that you in fact long for nothing,
and no one needs pity.

Yet I see you pouring red wine in the dark
and know you feel something
like a white embrace of arms rising behind you.
And the fear that nothing is really there
makes your blood miss and go cold.

Inside your chest there are hawks
that sink their claws into your heart,
try to fly off with it,
and you would like to let them go.
But soon the neighbor's chickens
will go mute around their eggs;

soon, it will be Monday
and we must let go of sleep,
go out where faces are blank and torn as clouds,
and it's not our fault.

for Mary Croal

In starched corduroy, navyblue and grey checked
                                                    shirts
we processed each Spring, sang hymns to The Blessed
                                                    Mother:
Mary Star Of The Sea, Regina Coeli Queen Of The Sky,
"Guide us by night, keep us by day, save us from
                                                    harm."

Flower girls threw petals from silver baskets--
petals of the milk-glass rose, petals holy and white
as the priest's vestments, the statue's flowering heart,
petals thin and pure as the girl's lace ankle socks.

The nun snapped a tin frog-clicker to genuflect
and when we were caught dreaming past the signal
her eyes fixed us with a fiery blue, like the sun
through Christ's robes in the window of The
                                                    Ascension;
and we were warned of the black jeopardy in our
                                                    souls.
We preened the grey feathers from our venial hearts
and raised our heads to gold--gold flame of beeswax,
gold of the ten-fingered Monstrance
where the Host was shown for life everlasting.

At 12 years old we thought nothing would end
and it was easy to believe it all.
Growing older, our mothers did our praying for us,
held onto the beads and repeated all the mysteries
to keep us from the fires.

But today I wonder if prayer or anything
parts the blank window of the earth or saves a life.

I saw the cancer like the dark cells of sin
that blemished our chalk-slate souls.
I saw clouds, strung like a rosary your empty house
prayed alone, thin-out into a row of thorns.

Where I live the water is deep blue
and grey-flecked with wind--the only light
floats from the oil platforms green as fog.
Mary, we believe what we believe, but who knows
we're not somewhere lost out on this ocean?

for Gary Soto

Last days of Lent and they're burning
in orange groves back of Anaheim.
Humus and citrus acid oil the air
redolent as incense; I recall the Miserere,
the 51st Psalm for mercy, we sang
before the curtained faces of the saints.
But nothing saves the growers, the orchards,
the water prayed-out the ditch's end.
They give in, a root to hard ground--
ash and a forecast of ash on what they breathe.

*   *

A hand of wind guts clouds to fishbones--
content to rent our homes,
we did not despair,
but took each winter's sun face value,
the sulphured valley air; we took wives,
our luck pressed on houses
repeating like shaved dice,
our breath coming short
with the weight of it all--
30, and half the promise gone.

*   *

6:00 and a priest pacing the garden
says his Office--hands pale as his Breviary pages,
his hair the dull water

of my father's and his before him,
that moth and rust beginning at mine.
He doesn't work the dirt for flowers
or see his prayers scatter like leaves
gone to pieces on the bare paths.
Doves wing on the bells for Angelus
and now the clouds are nothing more
than grey roads we look up each day
for a way to begin again.

*   *

Good Friday, a bird flies against the window--
smudge on the glass, vague lozenge
warning death if he gets in; and
the laundry, damp and heavy in my arms, drops.
The bird bleats away in a coma of sunlight.
November, 600 starlings fell
across San Luis Obispo, thudding
in the moonlight like bad fruit--
they ate grain sprayed routinely in the Fall.
Something cold over the heart as sleep,
thick as silver under thumbs
lets us shuck and bleed the air,
take everything we find under the sun.

3:00, pealing bells, a light rain ending
and we are moved to believe
a new season could be here. . .
The sun slurs, faint as a Communion Host
the priest carries to back the dying;
neighbors' dogs chorus in with sirens

and it's the same 6s and 7s.
Rain comes to little and the season less.
Mornings I wake and see spurred petals
of impatiens, each one with its "touch-me-not,"
and fewer blossoms of the orange white unguent
past the windfall and the final say.

What I've lost, I've lost for good--
sepals of the iris shedding like skin
and this week before summer,
the last pause and breath-holding of heart
before I must move once more. I slump
in a lawn chair, a gear turning by itself;
the clock says two and I wait
for the calls of birds to die in the heat.

What has passed will leave me
like the splinter working its way from my hand,
or the phases of the moon filling to darkness;
but it all follows in the long face of dreams.

I know this time by the white nettle crowning
pods of eucalyptus, half the lance-like leaves
drying to a bronze-red, and above the trees
a ragged fabric of clouds at twilight.
I remember the poem going,
"When I started home *I* darkness was gliding west."

Daylight pulls across the table and deeper
to where I imagine the ocean is calling.
Again, it is the easing away of things--
I have let my body go and become lonely,
but it will pass with the afternoons,
this week of living slowly, so little. . .

Bark is peeling from the branches
and I think of flesh sagging from bone,
Jesus hanging there, folding into himself,
blank eyes turning to a blank sky
after the bruised wine offered on a rag
and seven words sounding out for home.